W9-AVT-375

2006
NATIONAL FOOTBALL LEAGUE
MEGASTARS

by JOE LAYDEN

SCHOLASTIC INC.

New York   Toronto   London   Auckland   Sydney
Mexico City   New Delhi   Hong Kong   Buenos Aires

COVER PHOTO CREDITS
Smith: Jonathan Daniel/NFL Photos. **Alexander:** Otto Greule, Jr./NFL Photos.
Johnson: Andy Lyons/NFL Photos. **Bruschi:** David Maxwell/NFL Photos. **Simms:** Doug Benc/NFL Photos.

No part of this publication may be reproduced in whole or in part, or stored in a retrieval system, or transmitted in any form or by any means, electronic, mechanical, photocopying, recording, or otherwise, without written permission of the publisher. For information regarding permission, write to Scholastic Inc., Attention: Permissions Department, 557 Broadway, New York, NY 10012.

ISBN 0-439-82816-3

Copyright © 2006 NFL Properties LLC. Team name/logos are trademarks of the team indicated. All other NFL-related trademarks are trademarks of the National Football League.

Published by Scholastic Inc. All rights reserved. SCHOLASTIC, APPLE PAPERBACKS, and associated logos are trademarks and/or registered trademarks of Scholastic Inc.

12 11 10 9 8 7 6 5 4 3 2   6 7 8 9 10/0

Printed in the U.S.A.
First printing, August 2006
Book design by Michael Malone

Shaun
ALEXANDER

SHAUN ALEXANDER

RUNNING BACK
SEATTLE SEAHAWKS

BORN: 8/30/77
HEIGHT: 5-11
WEIGHT: 225
COLLEGE: ALABAMA

"You have to **see**
something happen
before you do it. I don't know
how you can **break records**
without seeing yourself
breaking them."

Most valuable player. Success is nothing new for Shaun Alexander. This, after all, is an athlete who once held the national record for most touchdowns by a high school player! Great things have been expected of Shaun since the day he entered the NFL, and he hasn't disappointed. With a sturdy, muscular build, and great field vision, Shaun quickly became one of the league's top offensive players after arriving in Seattle from the University of Alabama. But in 2005 he raised his game to a new level. Shaun rushed for 1,880 yards and scored 28 touchdowns. Along the way he became the first player in NFL history to score at least 15 touchdowns in five consecutive seasons. He also became the Seahawks' all-time leading rusher. If you ask Shaun, though, he'll tell you that his biggest accomplishment was helping Seattle to a 13-3 regular-season record—and a shot at the Super Bowl title. No wonder Shaun was voted the league's MVP. It's hard to imagine a player being more valuable!

Tiki
BARBER

© Al Bello/NFL Photos

TIKI BARBER

RUNNING BACK
NEW YORK GIANTS

BORN: 4/7/75
HEIGHT: 5-10
WEIGHT: 200
COLLEGE: VIRGINIA

"My career has been **so long** because I've been **reinvented** so many times."

Better with age. There's no such thing as an easy position in the NFL, but running backs in particular play a physically demanding role week after week. That's why it's unusual to see one who gets better the older he gets — especially after he hits thirty. So how do you explain Tiki Barber? Answer: you don't. You just shake your head in awe. Slowly but surely, Tiki has developed into one of the NFL's most durable and dependable running backs. At an age when most players are contemplating retirement, he's setting records! Tiki gained less than 1,000 yards—total—during his first three seasons in the league. Compare that to the fall of 2005, when he rushed for a team-record 1,860 yards, scored 11 touchdowns and had 2,390 total yards from scrimmage! He was also named to the Pro Bowl for the second straight season. Tiki's secret is a strenuous off-season training routine that helps keep him in peak shape. He's only 5-10, which is small for an NFL running back. But he carries a lot of muscle on his frame. And, of course, there is no questioning the size of Tiki's heart.

Tedy
BRUSCHI

© David Maxwell/NFL Photos

TEDY BRUSCHI

LINEBACKER
NEW ENGLAND PATRIOTS

BORN: 6/9/73
HEIGHT: 6-1
WEIGHT: 247
COLLEGE: ARIZONA

"**I'm a football player.**
That's what I do.
So I did **everything
I could** to make myself
a football player again."

Never count him out. Football players learn to live with injuries and time away from the game. It's all part of the job. But few athletes have faced the obstacles placed in front of Tedy Bruschi. In the winter of 2005, just two weeks after helping the Patriots win their third Super Bowl title in four years, Tedy suffered a minor stroke. It seemed an unlikely problem for someone so young and strong, and in such great physical condition. But Tedy had to face reality: he needed surgery to repair a small hole in his heart. Doctors told him he was lucky to be alive, and that he might never play football again. Tedy accepted the diagnosis, but in the back of his mind he believed that eventually he would return to the field. He worked hard in the off-season to get in shape. He took care of himself. And by the end of October he was back in the Patriots' lineup, sparking the defense as usual with his talent and spirit. Tedy's return to the field was one of the most uplifting stories of the 2005 season. It's no surprise that he was named co-winner of the NFL's Comeback Player of the Year Award.

Top: © Jim McIsaac/NFL Photos. Bottom: © Doug Pensinger/NFL Photos

Derrick
BURGESS

© Jim McIsaac/NFL Photos

DERRICK BURGESS

DEFENSIVE END
OAKLAND RAIDERS

BORN: 8/12/78
HEIGHT: 6-2
WEIGHT: 260
COLLEGE: MISSISSIPPI

"I wanted to **prove something** to myself—not other people. I've come a **long way.**"

Sack leader. On the final day of the 2005 regular season, during a game against the New York Giants, Derrick Burgess burst into the backfield and smothered his old college teammate, quarterback Eli Manning. It was the 16th time that Burgess had sacked a quarterback, breaking the single-season Oakland Raider team record in that category. Manning would later say that he wasn't surprised at his friend's emergence as one of the league's top pass rushers. After all, they had played together. Manning knew all about Derrick's cat-like quickness, and explosiveness at the line of scrimmage. Those traits had made Derrick a prized draft pick coming out of college, but a series of injuries had prevented him from reaching his potential. In fact, Derrick played in just one game during a two-year stretch with the Philadelphia Eagles. But since coming to Oakland in 2004, Derrick has been healthy and happy. That's good news for Raiders fans, and bad news for the rest of the NFL!

Top: © Jonathan Ferrey/NFL Photos. Bottom: © NFL Photos

Larry **FITZGERALD**

© Ronald Martinez /NFL Photos

11

LARRY FITZGERALD

WIDE RECEIVER
ARIZONA CARDINALS

BORN: 8/31/83
HEIGHT: 6-3
WEIGHT: 221
COLLEGE: PITTSBURGH

"For me, playing in the **NFL** is a **dream come true.**"

Playing with the big boys.

Sometimes it's hard to believe that Larry Fitzgerald has been playing professional football for just two years. Ask anyone in the NFL and they'll tell you that Larry is one of the smoothest receivers they've ever seen. Tall and lean, with a long, graceful stride and great leaping ability, he makes the impossible seem effortless. It's almost as if Larry was born to play in the NFL. That isn't quite the case, but it is true that Larry got an earlier start than most. When he was just 14 years old, Larry was a ball boy for the Minnesota Vikings. Not only would he study the moves of All-Pro receivers like Randy Moss and Cris Carter, but sometimes he'd hang around after practice and play catch with them. Talk about getting a first-class education! Larry obviously learned his lessons well. He was runner-up for the Heisman Trophy at the University of Pittsburgh before being drafted by the Cardinals, who knew that he had the potential to be a special player. It hasn't

taken long for Larry to deliver on that promise. In just his second season he was voted to the Pro Bowl and caught an amazing 103 passes, good enough for a share of the league lead. Just imagine what Larry will do when he gets a little more experience under his belt.

Top: © Eliot J. Schechter/NFL Photos. Bottom: © Harry How/NFL Photos

Chad **JOHNSON**

© Andy Lyons/NFL Photos

CHAD JOHNSON

WIDE RECEIVER
CINCINNATI BENGALS

BORN: 1/9/78
HEIGHT: 6-1
WEIGHT: 192
COLLEGE: OREGON STATE

"I love this game. That's why I'm so emotional."

The entertainer.

It's easy to get the wrong idea about Chad Johnson. You might have seen him working on one of his infamous touchdown celebrations—like the "Riverdance"—and think he's showing off. But that's not the case. It's just that Chad is a free spirit who gets so wrapped up in the game of football that he can't help but express his emotion. Fans love his exuberance. Teammates and coaches love his talent and intensity. They see another side of Chad—the side that works harder than everyone else in practice. They see a man who is so committed to winning that he spends two or three nights a week sleeping at the Bengals' practice facility. The hard work has paid off for Chad, who in 2005 led the AFC in receiving for the third straight season. There is no effective way to cover Chad. He has great hands and blistering speed. So he tends to wind up in the end zone with alarming frequency. And, once there, he likes to express his happiness. But don't be fooled. When it comes to football, Chad Johnson is all business.

Larry JOHNSON

© Larry W. Smith/NFL Photos

LARRY JOHNSON

RUNNING BACK
KANSAS CITY CHIEFS

BORN: 11/19/79
HEIGHT: 6-1
WEIGHT: 230
COLLEGE: PENN STATE

"I'm not trying to
live up to somebody else's
expectations.
I'm trying to live up to
my own."

The natural.
If you saw the Chiefs beat the Cincinnati Bengals in the final game of the 2005 season, you saw the future. And the future has a name: Larry Johnson. It wasn't just that Larry rushed for 201 yards and cracked the 100-yard barrier for the ninth straight time. It wasn't even the fact that he broke the Chiefs' single-season rushing mark with 1,750 yards, which was best in the AFC. If you're a Chiefs fan, and you want something to get excited about, simply rewind the tape and take a look at Larry's 20th touchdown of the season. It came on a spectacular 14-yard run from scrimmage, during which he covered the width of the field—twice! Larry went left, spun away from a bewildered and frustrated defender, then reversed direction and sprinted all the way around the right side of the offensive line and into the end zone. Afterward, he didn't even seem to be breathing hard. But that's Larry: he makes everything look easy. And that's why things are looking good for the Chiefs.

Shawne MERRIMAN

SHAWNE MERRIMAN

LINEBACKER
SAN DIEGO CHARGERS

BORN: 5/25/84
HEIGHT: 6-4
WEIGHT: 272
COLLEGE: MARYLAND

"Anybody who goes as **high** as I did in the draft should expect to be a **game-changer,** point-blank."

Raw intensity. You have to feel sorry for anyone assigned the task of blocking Shawne Merriman. He's too quick for most offensive linemen, and much too powerful for a running back. In his first season in the NFL, Shawne made a habit of tossing aside any player who crossed his path. He brought a new level of intensity to the Chargers, and proved more than worthy of the nickname that he's carried since his college days: "Lights Out!" Although a pre-season injury prevented Shawne from getting into the starting lineup through the first half of the season, he came on strong in the last few months. He finished the year with 54 tackles and 10 sacks, including two against Peyton Manning as the Chargers knocked off the previously unbeaten Indianapolis Colts. Every game is like a highlight film for Shawne, who plays as hard as he can each time the ball is snapped. It's no wonder that he was voted the NFL's Defensive Rookie of the Year.

Jake PLUMMER

© Doug Pensinger/NFL Photos

JAKE PLUMMER

QUARTERBACK
DENVER BRONCOS

BORN: 12/19/74
HEIGHT: 6-2
WEIGHT: 212
COLLEGE: ARIZONA STATE

"I have made **plenty of mistakes** in my career. So I know how to **bounce back** from them."

Persistence pays off.

Back in the day, when Jake Plummer was a Heisman Trophy candidate at Arizona State, he earned the nickname "Jake the Snake." Why? Because Jake was so elusive that defenders could never get a hand on him. Time and again, he'd scramble out of trouble and find an open receiver. When Jake got to the NFL, though, he found himself playing on a team that wasn't very successful. Sometimes he tried to do too much. He threw a lot of interceptions, and the pressure was mounting. A lesser player might have wilted. But not Jake. He continued to work hard and improve. Today, after nearly a decade in the league, he's one of the NFL's toughest and most reliable quarterbacks. His natural leadership skills helped the Broncos knock off the two-time defending Super Bowl champion New England Patriots in the 2005 playoffs. Not since the great John Elway retired have Broncos fans had a quarterback who could do so much on the field. Jake has waited a long time for this opportunity. And now he's making the most of it.

Troy
POLAMALU

© Andy Lyons/NFL Photos

21

TROY POLAMALU

SAFETY
PITTSBURGH STEELERS

BORN: 4/19/81
HEIGHT: 5-10
WEIGHT: 212
COLLEGE: USC

"I don't like to be the
safety valve.
I'd rather be on the
front lines."

A man of action.

Will the real Troy Polamalu please stand up? Is he the man with the long, flowing hair that hasn't been trimmed in three years? Is he the man who throws his body all over the field with such passion and reckless abandon that teammates have given him the nickname "Tasmanian Devil"? Is he the hardest hitter in the NFL? Or is he a thoughtful, modest young man who rarely loses his temper, prefers reading to watching television, and speaks so softly that he can barely be heard? The answer, of course, is that Troy is all of those things. And much more. After three years as a strong safety in the NFL, Troy has developed a reputation for patrolling the defensive secondary with a ferocity matched by few players. He's a tough, physical player who doesn't mind contact, but who also has the speed to keep up with the game's top receivers. He plays every game as if it might be his last. Off the field, however, Troy is shy and sensitive. You might say he's a man who believes in letting his actions speak for themselves.

Top: © Brian Bahr/NFL Photos. Bottom: © Tom Pidgeon/NFL Photos

Chris SIMMS

© Scott Halleran/NFL Photos

CHRIS SIMMS

QUARTERBACK
TAMPA BAY BUCCANEERS

BORN: 8/29/80
HEIGHT: 6-4
WEIGHT: 220
COLLEGE: TEXAS

"I don't care about **getting hit.** As long as **I get the ball off,** I don't mind."

Like father, like son.
Can you imagine having a father who is an NFL superstar? How cool would that be? Well, pretty cool, as Chris Simms would be the first to admit. His dad, Phil Simms, led the New York Giants to a Super Bowl championship in 1986, and Chris used to spend a lot of time hanging out in the locker room with his dad. Talk about a great life! But when Chris grew up and became a quarterback, too, suddenly it wasn't so easy to be the son of Phil Simms. Even though he's been in the NFL only three years, people expect a lot from Chris. But that's all right, because he demands a lot from himself, too. Since taking over as the starting QB for the Bucs midway through the 2005 season, Chris has displayed the kind of toughness and determination that made his father so popular with fans and teammates. He's the kind of quarterback who is willing to stand in the pocket until a receiver gets open. In the face of the heaviest rush, he remains calm and focused. It's no wonder that Chris is at his best in tight games, as the clock winds down. He understands pressure, and he embraces it.

Steve
SMITH

© Streeter Lecka/NFL Photos

25

STEVE SMITH

WIDE RECEIVER
CAROLINA PANTHERS

BORN: 5/12/79
HEIGHT: 5-9
WEIGHT: 185
COLLEGE: UTAH

"Getting hurt was
the best thing
that could have
happened to me."

The comeback kid. Don't ever underestimate Steve Smith. He
may not be one of the biggest wide receivers in the NFL, but he's one of the
best. As he's repeatedly demonstrated in the last two years, he's also one of the
toughest. Steve was primed to have a breakout season in 2004. Unfortunately,
he suffered an injury in the opening game. A broken leg put Steve in a cast and
on the sideline for the entire season. But Steve didn't complain. He worked hard
to get back in shape, and by the time he reported to training camp in the sum-
mer of 2005, Steve was hungrier than ever. Running pass routes with devastating precision, and using his incredible speed to scorch defensive backs, Steve
put together a dream season for the Panthers. He led the league in
receiving yards (1,563) and was tied for first in receptions (103) and
touchdowns (12). "The Butterfly," as teammates sometimes call
Steve, was also named co-winner of the NFL's Comeback
Player of the Year award. It's an honor he deserved, but
one he'd rather not repeat. Steve would prefer to stay on
the field, where he's right at home.

Jason TAYLOR

© Andy Lyons/NFL Photos

27

JASON TAYLOR

DEFENSIVE END
MIAMI DOLPHINS

BORN: 9/1/74
HEIGHT: 6-6
WEIGHT: 255
COLLEGE: AKRON

"If you work a few years like **others won't,** you'll live the **rest of your life** like others can't."

Model of consistency.

After nine years in the NFL, all with the Miami Dolphins, it might be tempting to take Jason Taylor for granted. After all, Jason is not the kind of player who will do a victory dance after sacking the quarterback. He isn't prone to emotional outbursts or patting himself on the back. He just shows up every day and works as hard as he can. Quietly and effectively, he leads by example. With a devastating combination of size, strength and speed, Jason is one of the best pass rushers in the league. He's also capable of dropping away from the line of scrimmage and helping the Dolphins at linebacker. That's because he's quick enough to cover even the best receivers. Just put Jason in the game and tell him what you want him to do. He'll get the job done. If you want further evidence of Jason's reliability, just check out his trophy case. He's also been to the Pro Bowl four times. And if you're a Dolphins fan, don't worry. Jason shows no signs of slowing down anytime soon.

Top: © Marty Lyons/NFL Photos Bottom: © Eliot J. Schechter/NFL Photos

Nathan
VASHER

NATHAN VASHER

DEFENSIVE BACK
CHICAGO BEARS

BORN: 11/17/81
HEIGHT: 5-10
WEIGHT: 180
COLLEGE: TEXAS

"I feel like I have just as muc **right to the ball** as the offensive player."

The interceptor.

When Nathan Vasher came to Chicago from the University of Texas, it was expected that he'd eventually make an impact on the defensive side of the ball. This was a young man who finished his college career as the Longhorns' career leader in interceptions. But no one could have anticipated just how quickly Nathan would become a big-time NFL player. He roams the secondary like a hungry wolf in search of its next meal. And when the ball is in the air, he goes after it. Any receiver in Nathan's territory can expect to be challenged. That toughness helped Nathan finish in the top five in the NFL in interceptions in 2005, which led to an invitation to the Pro Bowl. But what really made Nathan a superstar was a single play that didn't even involve an interception. Or a pass, for that matter. In a game against the San Francisco 49ers, Nathan returned a missed field goal 108 yards for a touchdown! It was one of the most electrifying plays of the entire season, and the longest touchdown in NFL history. But that's Nathan. He's been in the league only two years, and already he's rewriting the record books!

Top: © Jonathan Daniel/NFL Photos; Bottom: © Jonathan Daniel/NFL Photos

DeMarcus WARE

© Jonathan Ferrey/NFL Photos

DEMARCUS WARE

LINEBACKER
DALLAS COWBOYS

BORN: 7/31/82
HEIGHT: 6-4
WEIGHT: 255
COLLEGE: TROY STATE

"I feel like I can **play any position** they want me to play."

Nowhere to run...nowhere to hide.

How do you stop an athlete like DeMarcus Ware? Just look at the guy. He's big, strong and incredibly fast. When he was a college player at Troy State, he could bench press more than anyone else on the team. Maybe that's not such a big surprise, considering DeMarcus is a linebacker. But he also had the fastest 40-yard dash time of any player on the team. And the highest vertical jump. No wonder NFL scouts were drooling at the prospect of drafting DeMarcus. This was a young man with unlimited potential. Well, after just one year in the NFL, DeMarcus is already starting to realize some of that potential. He was smooth on pass coverage, and an overwhelming force when blitzing into the backfield. DeMarcus played one of his best games late in the year, recording three sacks and forcing three fumbles as the Cowboys kept their playoff hopes alive with an emotional victory over the Carolina Panthers. It was the type of performance that made you realize just how talented DeMarcus is. Imagine what he'll be like in a few years!

Top: © Otto Greule, Jr./NFL Photos. Bottom: © NFL Photos